IN THE
NATIONAL INTEREST

T0307216

General Sir John Monash once exhorted a graduating class to 'equip yourself for life, not solely for your own benefit but for the benefit of the whole community'. At the university established in his name, we repeat this statement to our own graduating classes, to acknowledge how important it is that common or public good flows from education.

Universities spread and build on the knowledge they acquire through scholarship in many ways, well beyond the transmission of this learning through education. It is a necessary part of a university's role to debate its findings, not only with other researchers and scholars, but also with the broader community in which it resides.

Publishing for the benefit of society is an important part of a university's commitment to free intellectual inquiry. A university provides civil space for such inquiry by its scholars, as well as for investigations by public intellectuals and expert practitioners.

This series, In the National Interest, embodies Monash University's mission to extend knowledge and encourage informed debate about matters of great significance to Australia's future.

Professor Margaret Gardner AC
President and Vice-Chancellor,
Monash University

KATE THWAITES & JENNY MACKLIN

ENOUGH IS ENOUGH

MONASH
UNIVERSITY
PUBLISHING

Enough Is Enough
© Copyright 2021 Kate Thwaites and Jenny Macklin

Monash University Publishing
Matheson Library Annexe
40 Exhibition Walk
Monash University
Clayton, Victoria 3800, Australia
https://publishing.monash.edu

Monash University Publishing brings to the world publications which advance the best traditions of humane and enlightened thought.

ISBN: 9781922464699 (paperback)
ISBN: 9781922464705 (ebook)

Series: In the National Interest
Editor: Louise Adler
Project manager & copyeditor: Paul Smitz
Designer: Peter Long
Typesetter: Cannon Typesetting
Proofreader: Gillian Armitage
Printed in Australia by Ligare Book Printers

A catalogue record for this book is available from the National Library of Australia.

The paper this book is printed on is in accordance with the standards of the Forest Stewardship Council®. The FSC® promotes environmentally responsible, socially beneficial and economically viable management of the world's forests.

To all of our colleagues in parliament who know there is no place for the abuse of women, and who speak out, campaign, and change laws to protect women and punish perpetrators, we hope this book strengthens each of you.

PREFACE

On the Monday morning of a sitting week in March 2021, I stood with fellow members of parliament and thousands of angry women on the lawns outside Parliament House in Canberra, listening as former political staffer Brittany Higgins detailed her experience of being raped inside the building two years earlier. Framed against the big white edifice, she spoke with extraordinary clarity:

> There is a confronting sense of banality about sexual violence in our community. I was raped inside Parliament House by a colleague and for so long it felt like the people around me only cared because of where it happened and what it might mean for them. It was so

confusing because these people were my idols. I had dedicated my life to them. They were my social network, my colleagues and my family. And suddenly they treated me differently. I wasn't a person who had just gone through a lifechanging traumatic event. I was a political problem.[1]

To me, the speech was almost too painful to hear, and I can't really fathom the bravery and resilience that Brittany Higgins drew on to speak those words. However, at that moment, one thing did seem evident—her clarity and her courage demanded immediate action. Our parliament and our country felt close to breaking point. The courage shown by Brittany Higgins and by 2021 Australian of the Year Grace Tame in publicly telling their stories had brought forward women across the country to also share theirs. We were all demanding change.

Then I walked into the building, my workplace, to the madness of a Question Time where the voices of the multitude outside had not been heard inside.

Prime Minister Morrison explained to the protesting women that it was a triumph of democracy that they had not been shot, then mumbled his way through a shopping list of 'Australian Government reports' that had something to do with women, to try to demonstrate that things were being fixed.[2]

The treatment of women's horrific experiences of sexual violence as a political problem, which had just been called out so powerfully by Brittany Higgins and had prompted thousands of women to march on Parliament House, was to continue unabated. The most powerful man in politics had just confirmed it. And I was furious. What would it take for enough to be enough?

How is it that the political power we need to wield to change the country has also been used to damage so many women who work in our legislature? Why are so many Australian women still experiencing sexual violence and harassment in their workplaces? Has anything fundamentally changed in our community in the almost eight decades since women were first elected to the Australian Parliament?

This book is an attempt by myself and Jenny, as a current and a former member of parliament respectively, to understand and explain what it is about the culture, structure and practices of Parliament House that has allowed sexual violence and harassment to flourish there, and why Australian women still encounter violence and discrimination across the breadth of this country's workplaces and communities. We have written this as women who believe in the power of politics to do good, and as feminists.

Jenny was a Labor MP for twenty-three years, twenty-two of which were spent as a Cabinet or shadow cabinet minister, and she now gets to view parliament through the reflective eyes of someone who is no longer there. I'm in my first term as a Labor MP. There is a generation between the beginning of Jenny's time in parliament and mine. When she was first elected in 1996, to represent the Victorian division of Jagajaga, I was in my final years of high school; I would not enter parliament myself until 2019. In the period between Jenny being elected and me being elected, the number of women in the Australian Parliament increased from forty-six to eighty-three. It is now much more common for women to be in the room where the decisions are made. Unfortunately, they still are not always heard when they should be. And tragically, they are not always safe.

Jenny and I both feel the weight of responsibility of having a privileged voice and of being part of a political class that has not yet delivered equality for the women of this country. We are Labor women, but we don't excuse our side of politics from culpability. Ultimately, politics is about power. Women wielding power in Parliament House, women fighting for equality and an end to discrimination across our country, have made their mark; they have improved women's lives. But the underlying problem of men's attitude towards women, of men believing it is their right to assault or harass women, remains. For this to change, we need structures, policies and consequences that will cause men to stop using power in harmful ways—in the parliament, and in the community, too.

We are calling for consequences for actions and an end to the culture of political impunity. We want to seize this moment to complete the unfinished work for Australian women—to make sure that women are not just in the room but are safe there and clearly heard; to have women wield power to change the laws that have allowed men to escape responsibility for their violence against women; and to change harmful gender norms from the very beginning of a child's life.

Enough is enough.

ENOUGH IS ENOUGH

When Jenny and I started talking about all these issues, the first phenomenon we remarked on was the physicality of Parliament House. The place is huge. The House of Representatives, where we MPs debate, is cavernous—during a rowdy Question Time, when the chamber is full, it feels as though a wall of sound is hitting you. It is an environment seemingly best suited to the biggest bodies and the loudest voices.

Jenny tells me how she used to sit between Lindsay Tanner and Mark Latham during Question Time: 'I felt like a squashed ant.' I sit up the back of the chamber, where my voice doesn't carry or cut through the noise. If I ask the Prime Minister a question, he doesn't look at me when he answers. And the heckling from the other side can sometimes seem designed to play on any insecurities you might have about whether you belong. I remember being jeered during one speech by a man about my age. 'You're new here,' he said. 'You don't get it.'

Jenny says she used to be told: 'Get back onto your broomstick.' At the time she just laughed it off, but reflecting on it now, she has a slightly different take: 'As women find everywhere, complaining just shows you aren't a good sport, you don't have a sense of humour. I know that the reason I laughed things off was because I didn't want to be defined by complaining.'

In this, Jenny is backed up by Sex Discrimination Commissioner Kate Jenkins, who in a speech to the National Press Club in 2016 remarked:

> As a culture in Australia we are indoctrinated
> to believe we are an 'easygoing' nation, one that
> can take a joke, and one that doesn't much like
> whingers. Toughness and resilience are highly
> valued … As a result, it is only the privileged

few who are in a position where they can speak up without fear of the consequences. This means the victims speak up at their own peril … And instead, they have learned to stay silent.[3]

I think the issue here for women is not just the expectation that you'll laugh it off, but also the constant niggling feeling that because there aren't as many of you, you may not really belong. In the WhatsApp group I share with some new female MPs, one of our frequently voiced small frustrations is the way in which security guards constantly mistake us for staffers or visitors, something we don't notice happening to male MPs—the ones who stride the corridors pretending to be extras on *The West Wing*, the ones who look how people expect a politician to look.

Of course, there are the public judgements of how a politician should look, and what they should be like as well. These judgements can seem particularly pointed and vicious when directed at females, particularly the comments made online about our appearance and our family choices. I had one visitor to my Facebook page comment on a photo of me holding my daughter, asking if I'd had a C-section because he thought my stomach made it look like I had. I don't think he was a medical professional.

My fellow Labor MP Anne Aly gave a speech in parliament in March 2021 in which she explained how the abuse she receives is next-level for her as a woman and as a Muslim:

> All women deserve to feel safe in public, in workplaces, in their homes. Criminal or abhorrent behaviour and comments directed at women is a serious issue that needs urgent action, and members of parliament are not immune.
>
> I shall refrain from using some of the more disgusting language as I read out some of the comments I have received. One user wrote: 'I can't wait till Fraser Anning is our new Fuhrer and you will be sent to the ovens. One day soon we will be at your doorstep. We will

take you and your family away to be loaded on a carriage. I can't wait for the Final Solution—train carriages packed full of Muslims heading to the ovens. It will be truly wonderful.'

I have somebody who regularly writes to me addressing his letters to the 'ISIS whore', sending me vile racist material directed at Labor female MPs. Enough is enough.[4]

And then there's the away-from-home, don't-ask-don't-tell environment. When federal parliament sits, most of the MPs, ministers and staffers in the building are away from home. It feels a bit like what I imagine boarding school must be like, with the same people interacting for hours on end in a confined space (often without actually seeing daylight), operating under a set of arcane and opaque rules. Then, once it hits 5 p.m., there are numerous functions put on by various lobby groups, all of them serving alcohol. The Sex Discrimination Commissioner's very thorough national inquiry into sexual harassment in Australian workplaces lists the use of alcohol as one of the cultural and systemic factors that greatly contribute to the prevalence of workplace sexual harassment.[5]

And when you leave Parliament House, you don't go home to your ordinary domestic demands. There is no partner telling you about their day or asking you why you forgot to buy more nappies. There's no toddler waiting to be wrangled into the bath. Instead, work and the power plays of the environment can become all-consuming. Sam Mostyn, a former parliamentary staffer who is now the president of Chief Executive Women, describes it like this:

> Because of the unique nature of it as a workplace, it's unlike any other place really in the country. When I worked there, I always used to think about entering a spaceship that had no relevance to anything happening outside it within the geography of Canberra, let alone the country. Because it's a place where very different things happen, it's a heady mixture of power, and quite a lot of desire

I think; there's lots of young people. I think most people going into that building who are not the permanent workers spend twenty-two weeks away from their family so it's very much a 'fly in, fly out' venue, which we don't often think about … [in] the way we think about FIFO workplaces elsewhere. There are very late hours, there's huge pressure, there's constant media interaction.[6]

Liberal frontbencher Karen Andrews says, 'It is quite exclusive here in Parliament. It's not an inclusive environment for women … the impact is that many women here do feel quite socially isolated, we aren't included in many of the discussions that happen …'[7]

The majority of these things in themselves are not crimes. But when I think about what creates a culture where sexual crimes can occur, the fact that women often feel uncertain about their place, that they feel devalued, is likely to be a contributing factor. This can also allow men to believe that their actions have no consequences.

And what about the staffers, the people who are in a much more vulnerable position than the ministers or MPs? The way in which the people in ministerial and MP offices are employed means that staffers really have nowhere independent to turn to when they need to raise allegations of assault, or harassment, or problems with the workplace culture. Their boss has a political interest in making sure such allegations do not become public or create any waves. The structures set up under the Department of Finance are the only other avenue for employees to take, but these were intended to deal with the very different workplace environment of the public service.

Jobs in politics are necessarily personal. The offices are small, the hours gruelling, and absolute trust between staffer and boss is essential. But this means that ministers and MPs tend to employ the people they feel most comfortable around—people who look like them, sound like them, even think like them. The situation in a parliament where we still have more elected men than women, and where men hold most of the senior positions within the federal government, often translates into similar gender imbalances in the ministerial and parliamentary offices.

I've worked as a staffer—I worked for Jenny when she was a federal minister in the Gillard government. But my experiences of parliament's harassment culture are observational rather than personal. I was nearly thirty when I walked in, having already negotiated the power and gender dynamics of the media industry, where I worked as a radio and television journalist. In fact, my staffer experiences tended not towards discrimination or harassment but to seeing up close what can be achieved when powerful women are first and foremost in a government running the country. And that is a large part of why I am now back in the parliament as an MP. But it is clear that my experience has not been the experience of many past and current women staffers in parliament.

A woman who has worked as a parliamentary staffer for nearly a decade explains it to me like this: 'When I first moved to Canberra as an enthusiastic 24-year-old, I was ill-equipped for dealing with the predatory nature of this environment. I have been objectified and sexually harassed by male staffers, I have had my breast grabbed by a senior colleague and my leg rubbed under a table. I have felt pressured to engage in sexual relationships with married and partnered men who held power over me professionally. My agency and autonomy slowly eroded.

'On reflection, my behaviour over the past decade has not been perfect. I'm not proud of all my actions. I have internalised the misogyny of this place, and I believe I was groomed to accept the poor behaviour of male MPs and staffers. Now, when I look back at certain interactions and experiences where I thought I was in control or being a "team player", I can see I was being manipulated and exploited.

'There is a difference between feeling empowered and having power. Parliament House is an environment that thrives off micro-aggressions, ego and power. The misogyny at times can be so subtle that in my direct experience as a young female staffer, I was conditioned to not speak unless spoken to. I quickly learnt from the conversations senior men had in my presence that there were two types of women in this place: those who were "cool girls" who could handle a joke, and the "nerdy policy wonks" who were too serious or caused an annoyance when they challenged or questioned senior men.'

The culture of our national parliament has permitted and encouraged a power imbalance and allowed men to behave with a sense of impunity, free from consequences for bad and potentially criminal behaviour. In the main, I think women have felt they needed to remain quiet about the problems with the parliamentary culture in order to operate within it. But the power of those young women who have spoken up about their experiences, about their treatment, most notably Brittany Higgins, is changing the dynamic of silence.

WOMEN IN THE HOUSE

Women aren't a new feature of our legislature. It has been a century since the first woman was elected to an Australian parliament, with Edith Cowan having attained the Western Australian Legislative Assembly in 1921. Then, in 1943, Dorothy Tangney and Dame Enid Lyons became the first women to be elected to the federal parliament. During that recent crazy March parliamentary sitting fortnight, I and my colleagues Alicia Payne and Anika Wells paid tribute to these two trailblazing women by recreating the historic photo of them entering Old Parliament House, with the flourish that we walked into Parliament House holding our babies. We'd all just returned from parental leave, something that would have been unimaginable in Tangney and Lyons' time.

It's at this point that I have to assert that which Jenny is most concerned for us to get across in this book: positive change for women does happen. Change in recent decades, for instance, without doubt has improved the lives of women in Australia. Now, we can and we should push for even greater change for greater benefits for women in our parliament and across our country.

There have been times over the past few months when Australian women have felt exhausted, when they have despaired. I know that many of my colleagues have struggled with the terrible allegations of what has occurred in Parliament House, and with a feeling of responsibility for what else they could have done and what more they can actually do now. Jenny has been told by many of her feminist friends that they feel like their work has been in vain, that they have failed the generation of women who came after them. As someone who is ever focused on what she has achieved and still can achieve, Jenny vigorously disagrees with this.

'I first became a feminist in the early 1970s,' she tells me. 'Change was underway with the wave of activists from the 1960s and then the seventies. We faced the culture of the time that women's place was in the home. We did not have legal control over our bodies. Abortion was a crime. Discrimination was rife everywhere. Women were paid lower rates of pay for the same work when working alongside men. Our babies were taken away if we gave birth when we were single.

All these matters were at the heart of our campaigns for change. We wanted women to be able to get away from violent partners and to change the laws about rape. Many of the issues have seen positive change. Women can now access contraception on the Pharmaceutical Benefits Scheme, abortion is legal, we have national paid parental leave and sex discrimination legislation.'

This proves an excellent prompt for me to do some research on the introduction of the *Sex Discrimination Act*. I must admit that, despite understanding how important this legislation has been for Australian women, as someone who was born in 1980 I have been largely unaware of just how controversial its introduction was. Here's a very brief history.

The *Sex Discrimination Act* became law in 1984 under the Hawke government. The Sex Discrimination Bill was introduced by senator Susan Ryan, then the minister assisting the prime minister for the status of women and the only woman in Cabinet. Much of it was drawn from a private member's bill she had introduced in the

Senate in 1981 while in opposition. The objective of that bill was to make discrimination illegal on the grounds of sex, marital status or pregnancy. It also outlawed sexual harassment in the workplace, marking the first time in Australia that such protection had been legislated. The Commonwealth bill built on provisions already in place in some states; extended coverage to all areas of employment, education and services; and included the new prohibitions on sexual harassment.[8]

The act's introduction was fiercely contested. Federal Liberal and National Party MPs were allowed a free vote on the bill, which was passed by the Senate by forty votes to twelve, and by the House of Representatives by eighty-six votes to twenty-six. Reflecting on the introduction of the bill twenty years later, Susan Ryan wrote:

> Parliament was besieged by thousands of petitions stating opposition to the Bill in the most colourful terms. Inside and outside Parliament, opponents claimed that the Bill would bring about the end of the family, ruin

the economy, undermine the male labour force and destroy Christianity and the Australian way of life.[9]

A glance through some of the newspaper articles of the time certainly backs this up, their headlines denouncing a law that would hurt the family, disenfranchise the housewife, and draw battlelines. I can't go past sharing part of a *Courier Mail* article titled 'Will We Be Allowed to Wink at a Woman?' In this piece, Sir James Killen, a former Liberal MP, essentially argues that the parliament was legislating in regard to areas where it had no place being. 'Is a wink at a bus conductress, the sending of flowers to a hostess, the helping of a woman across a street, "sexual harassment"?' he asks, before arguing that he has worked with lots of women and has always acknowledged their complete equality.[10] Sir James' anxiety about whether men would have to change their behaviour in response to legislative reform doesn't seem all that far away from some of the concerns male columnists are raising in the current debate.

Going back to Jenny's argument that changes have occurred in recent times that have improved the lives of Australian women, how does the *Sex Discrimination Act* fit into this? A 2008 Senate committee review noted that submissions to the inquiry were overwhelmingly supportive of the act and its objectives, representing a dramatic shift in public attitudes since the act's controversial passage in 1984. However, evidence presented to the committee suggested that while the act had impacted the most overt forms of sex discrimination, it had been less successful in addressing systemic discrimination.[11] The early months of 2021 can certainly attest to that.

Jenny and I have no doubt that one of the key reasons parliaments across Australia made the aforementioned changes is because more women had been elected to them, and therefore there were more women in parliament forcing the issues. The *Sex Discrimination Act* and other significant developments have come about because women like Susan Ryan have worked hard to get elected, then spoken out and agitated. So much of politics is about the numbers. Having greater numbers means you wield the power to be in the room, then the power to form government, and then you have the power to make laws that can change the country.

Jenny tells me there were several points in her parliamentary career when she realised the power inherent in having a significant number of women in the Labor Caucus. When these women took a united stand on an issue, it meant that the men in the party understood there were enough women who cared about the party's position that this might flow on and affect how they voted on things like internal leadership ballots. The power of numbers allowed women to exercise power over policy.

In his 2020 Budget reply, Opposition Leader Anthony Albanese made affordable child care the centrepiece of Labor's offering, with a $6 billion reform pledge.[12] It's a policy built on economics, targeting increased productivity by allowing those women who are currently locked out of the workforce by the prohibitive cost of child care to work more. I have absolutely no doubt that one of the reasons that affordable child care became front and centre in Labor's agenda for the country was because our team includes so many women, in particular so many senior women who are in the room when big political moments like the budget reply are put together—and also because we have so many men who are now used to having senior women in the room. Indeed, the shadow minister responsible for child care, Amanda Rishworth, has two children below five years of age. Lived experience makes a difference in both seeing and solving problems.

This is not to argue that all women want or need the same things, and that all women's politics are the same. There are fundamental differences between how Jenny and I want to use political power for change and how women in the Liberal Party look to shape our country. Rather, it is to demonstrate that women can and should wield political power to get outcomes, and that those outcomes can benefit women across the country. It is an argument for having more women elected so that we have the power of numbers behind us.

It is simply unacceptable that one Australian woman is killed on average every eight days at the hands of her current or former partner. It is unacceptable that, as shadow minister for Indigenous Australians Linda Burney puts it, 'the level of violence, the level of homicide, and the level of hospitalisation of First Nations women is almost indescribable'.[13] It is a tragedy of wasted opportunity that Australian women ranked first for educational attainment on the World Economic Forum's latest Global Gender Gap Index, but seventieth for economic participation and opportunity.

We need more women in parliament using the strength of our numbers to say that enough is enough. We can point out that we already know what changes we need to make to help keep women safe in our community—they are in the recommendations of the report into family, domestic and sexual violence produced by the Standing Committee on Social Policy and Legal Affairs in April 2021, and in those of the many inquiries that preceded it. We know many of the things that we

need to do to make women safe in the workplace—
they are contained in the *Respect@Work* report.
They just haven't been acted upon.

Then there's the power of numbers when it
comes to the culture of our parliament. I entered
a federal parliament where women made up
47 per cent of Labor's members and 23 per cent
of the Coalition's. That means there are women
around me who have shared some of those every-
day experiences of women in a workplace—of
being talked over in a meeting, of having their
ideas presented back to them more loudly by a
man, of spending probably way too much time
having to consider what our hair looks like and
whether we've packed enough changes of clothes.
It's why I'm part of that WhatsApp group of fellow
female MPs, an online space to vent, encourage
and support each other.

I'm also part of a baby boom on the Labor side
of politics. Since the 2019 federal election, Labor
women Amanda Rishworth, Lisa Chesters, Alicia
Payne, Anika Wells, Marielle Smith and I have all
had babies. Our male colleagues Patrick Gorman

and Matt Keogh have also supported their wives to grow new humans in this term of parliament. That March 2021 sitting fortnight that I keep referencing was when I returned to parliament with my three-month-old boy. I also brought my partner, Daniel, but I left my three-year-old daughter at home with her grandparents. As is known by the many women juggling work and caregiving, none of these decisions are easy. The guilt about whether I am doing enough for my children can hit me with great force at various times during a long parliamentary day. The feeling that I am missing important time with them hits me especially hard on the Wednesday morning of a sitting week, when that invisible string that ties us together seems close to snapping. Jenny says that leaving her children behind in Melbourne whenever she left for Canberra never stopped being a wrench during her more than two decades in politics.

While riding the sleep-deprived hormonal roller-coaster in the months after giving birth to my son, one of the main things that kept me going was knowing there were women around me going through the same thing and with whom I could share this experience, as well as knowing that women before me had been able to have a family and be a parliamentarian. Jenny says increased numbers of women in Parliament House is the biggest change she's seen there. 'It really does change the whole atmosphere,' she says. 'There were only four of us on our side in the House when I started. It's taken nearly thirty years for us to achieve what we set out to achieve with the quota decision in 1994.' That decision involved the Labor Party setting a rule that 35 per cent of winnable seats would be filled by women by 2002—the quota has since been raised.

'Once the decision is made on quotas, the change comes in each preselection round, and of course there is lots of male resistance,' Jenny says. 'Men don't want to retire, and there often seems to be some "brilliant" bloke who really should be preselected for the good of the party. The quotas are still contested. More than once I've heard rumblings about the so-called correct interpretation of the quota rules. If we hadn't introduced quotas, I'm absolutely convinced very few women would have been preselected.'

Other senior Labor women endorse Jenny's experience that having more females in the national parliament has changed the place. Tanya Plibersek, the Member for Sydney, tells me that women shouldn't have to police men's behaviour, and that it isn't necessarily the case that women always behave differently from men. But she says that she became an MP when around a quarter of parliamentarians were women, and that the place does feel different now that about half the elected representatives are women. She adds that more men are now more conscious of how they behave— although obviously not enough of them feel this weight of women's presence yet—and that she also gets a boost from knowing she has women around her who share her experiences.

I should acknowledge here that many of my male colleagues are appalled and shamed by the terrible allegations and disgusting behaviour involving our parliament. They too want a better culture, and above all for women to be safe at work.

CHANGING THE
PARLIAMENTARY CULTURE

Following up on Tanya's point that women shouldn't have to police men's behaviour, yes, having more women in parliament is vital, but the responsibility for change shouldn't rest solely with women. Fundamental cultural change in parliament will only happen when there are stronger structures in place to protect women, when there are strong consequences for men's actions, and when men change their behaviour.

Some of that structural change will involve reforming parliament as a workplace. This should include modernising our HR practices, bringing them into line with other Australian workplaces. There should be an independent someone that staffers can turn to for advice, counselling and support, to guarantee that all complaints are both taken seriously and dealt with appropriately. Just as in most other professional workplaces in Australia today, there should be ongoing training for ministers and MPs about what it means to be an employer and a leader, and about our professional responsibilities to our employees.

Australia's is not the only parliament to be confronted by these issues. The *Independent External Review into Bullying and Harassment in the New Zealand Parliamentary Workplace*, published in May 2019, identifies our neighbour's parliament as a workplace with a high-intensity culture. The reviewer, Debbie Francis, makes the point that, in contrast to other modern New Zealand workplaces, the country's parliament does not invest in workplace training and leadership development for MPs, and that while it may be a unique type of workplace, this is no excuse. She concludes:

> It is unusual to expect those in key leadership positions in a high-intensity, demanding workplace like Parliament, whether Members or corporate managers, to lead without systematic and framework driven professional development or support. I suggest that underinvestment in this area may exacerbate the other risks inherent in Parliament's unique culture.[14]

Dame Laura Cox's 2018 inquiry into the bullying and harassment of staff in the United Kingdom's House of Commons also has many themes in common with the Australian experience. Cox identifies a lack of support for staff who have been bullied, a culture that seeks to cover up harassment, an absence of accountability, and a lack of protection for staff who report abuse. Her report states that many people submitted the view that parliament was a unique institution and therefore should somehow be exempt from the norms of other workplaces. However, she determines that it is still a workplace where people are employed and so they are owed a duty of care.[15]

In response to that inquiry, and two others, the UK Parliament has undertaken a series of reforms, including establishing an independent expert panel to determine claims of bullying and harassment. MPs take no part in the panel's decision-making, and it has the power to determine sanctions should a case of bullying or harassment be upheld. If the panel recommends any of the most extreme sanctions, such as the suspension or expulsion of an MP, they must be approved by the House of Commons via a motion in the chamber.[16]

The Victorian Parliament is currently considering a model that seems similar to parts of the UK model, including a proposed independent commissioner who could impose sanctions on those MPs who are found to have bullied or harassed staff. The Speaker of the Victorian Legislative Assembly, Colin Brooks, told *The Age* there is a tendency for these matters to be viewed 'through a political prism', but the priority has to be the safety of staff. 'Members of Parliament are not above the law,' he says.[17]

Some reforms are already underway at the national level in Australia. At the time of writing, the Morrison government belatedly released its response to the *Respect@Work* report. That response did not include a commitment to act on the key recommendation that employers should have a positive duty to prevent sexual harassment in their workplaces. It did include a commitment to close a loophole in the *Sex Discrimination Act* that exempts MPs and judges from sexual harassment claims.[18] That is a step forward. But so far, the federal government has been hazy on what the consequences should be for MPs who are found to have breached the act.

Jenny and I are firmly of the belief that without serious consequences, the worst of the behaviour is unlikely to change. As in the United Kingdom, we should have a system to penalise MPs who are found to have engaged in sexual harassment, including the option of having them forced out of parliament.

The Labor Party, after reflecting on its own not-always-sterling record, has adopted three key new policies and procedures: a national policy for bullying and harassment prevention and response, a national code of conduct, and a national complaints handling process. The work done to develop these owes a lot to my colleague Sharon Claydon, who as Chair of Labor's Status of Women Caucus Committee and in her work across parliament, has always championed women. As yet, none of these new Labor policies have been tested in action. One of the biggest tests will be whether the consequences of not following these policies and procedures are serious enough to change behaviour.

YOU CAN'T BE WHAT YOU CAN'T SEE

We also need to change the way we conduct the politics of parliament, including how the public see us conduct it. Question Time is the most visible aspect of parliament for most Australians—glimpsed on the TV news at night, or when they visit Parliament House as schoolchildren—but it is also the environment we talked about earlier, where loud voices and big bodies seem to dominate. I can't help but think that this affects not just how women who are currently in parliament get heard and recognised, but also what women outside parliament think to themselves when they look at it: 'That place is not for me.' Reducing the testosterone level of Question Time may go some way towards changing this.

My colleague Peta Murphy and I were some of a number of MPs who made submissions to a recent parliamentary inquiry about how we might reform Question Time. One of the reasons we did so was because the feedback we get from observers is frequently amazement at a standard of behaviour that would not be tolerated in any other workplace. Some of the reforms we suggested to change the tone and conduct during Question Time were ending the practice of Dorothy Dixers, where a government minister is asked a question by a backbencher simply so that they can talk up their party's achievements; tightening the definition of 'relevance' to prevent gratuitous personal or partisan attacks; and prioritising portfolio-specific Question Times and constituency-specific questions, to allow backbenchers to ask ministers about issues relating to their electorate.

This is not to say that women can't be effective under the current rules of Question Time. A quick Twitter search for the words 'the Member for Jagajaga' will tell you that Jenny was very effective at cutting through Question Time noise with interjections during her time in parliament—so effective that she was routinely warned by the speaker about it! And it was during Question Time that Julia Gillard delivered her most famous speech as prime minister, which included the line addressed to Tony Abbott, 'I will not be lectured by this man!' Other women in parliament use various techniques to make their points. But it is the case that Question Time makes many women outside parliament (and some of those inside it) wonder why they would want to be a part of it.

Another way of making parliament more family-friendly, as well as more accessible to people of diverse backgrounds, is by cementing the use of remote facilities for MPs who have caregiving responsibilities. For much of 2019, the COVID-prompted Victorian lockdown meant that I was a virtual parliamentarian. The ACT Government requirement for me getting to Canberra in person was a two-week hotel quarantine period, but I was pregnant and had a toddler at home, so I couldn't realistically do this. The fact that our parliamentary rules were changed to allow me to advocate on behalf of my community via a video link from my electorate office made a world of difference to me.

Beyond the time of COVID, the ability to use a video link to participate in proceedings would help parliamentarians continue to do their jobs when caregiving responsibilities or personal illness mean they are unable to get to Canberra.

The conversations we had as MPs about setting up remote facilities were serious ones. Many felt the weight of practice and the history of parliament in contemplating whether a remote presence should be permitted. When I talked about it with people in my community, though, they were bemused about why we took so long to work it out. Their workplaces had moved to a virtual model almost immediately at the start of the pandemic, and many continue with a hybrid work model today.

The Westminster parliament, from where Australia draws many of its traditions and procedures, applied an even more extensive version of remote political work during the pandemic. The Centenary Action Group, which works to have more women included in British politics and which studied this period in the United Kingdom, has urged a continuation of the hybrid model rather than a return to business as usual. In particular, it highlights how conversations about what normal might look like in the post-pandemic world must not ignore questions of inclusiveness and diversity:

> The images seen of MPs participating remotely, sitting at their kitchen tables in front of their microwaves, may work to demystify and normalize the job of an MP. If we combine this with a knowledge that, if needed, one would be able to participate remotely, this could transform who considers themselves able to fulfil the job of an MP. In particular, benefits will be seen for those with caring responsibilities, who live far from Westminster, who have long-term or fluctuating health conditions, or are bereaved.[19]

Those points about demystifying the job and transforming who considers themselves able to fulfil the role of an MP are important ones in the Australian context. Our national parliament is not only mainly male, it's pale (I've left out 'stale' as

I don't think that's necessarily fair). The reality is that only a small group of people see themselves reflected in our parliament. That means there is only a small group of people who consider themselves likely to become parliamentarians, and who know who can help get them preselected and then elected.

Tasmanian Senator Jacqui Lambie argues that the problem with the parliamentary culture is not sexism but elitism. Writing about the way in which Brittany Higgins was treated, Senator Lambie describes how many politicians dress the same ('three pairs of black RM Williams boots') and how many went to the same private schools and prestigious universities. She says that

> when you think you're the most important person in the world, the most gifted and most fantastic person the Parliament has ever known, I reckon it's possible to see how you'd find a way to take the mistreatment of a young staff member in your office and make it completely about you.[20]

I'm very conscious that Jenny and I are writing this book as white, heterosexual women; that our experience is not the universal experience of all women, that it is more privileged than that of many; that as well as more women in our parliament, we need more women from diverse backgrounds—more First Nation women, like my amazing colleagues Linda Burney and Malarndirri McCarthy.

Jenny points out the work of Kate Manne, who in her book *Entitled: How Male Privilege Hurts Women* unpicks how male privilege and entitlement operate to keep women in their place, and how that dynamic frequently inter-sects with racism. Manne writes about how 'an illegitimate sense of male entitlement gives rise to a wide range of misogynistic behavior', where women are punished for not giving a man what he is tacitly deemed entitled to, and that misogyny is inextricably bound up with related social ills, so that an intersectional approach which considers racism, xenophobia, classism, homophobia, transphobia and ableism, among other things, is required.[21] It's a strong argument for why the fight for the improvement of women's lives can't just be a fight for the improvement of privileged women's lives.

Greater diversity in our parliament would mean we would be better at fighting for the improvement of the lives of *all* women, that we would represent Australia as a whole. It would make what can be a toxic and damaging culture within Parliament House seem less normal and be less acceptable. It would bring a greater focus in our politics on the treatment of women across our community. Making it easier for women from diverse backgrounds to enter parliament must be a priority.

Jenny reminds me that there is a precedent for changing the rules governing how parliament operates, so as to make it possible for many more women to see themselves, and their lives, reflected in parliamentary practice. It was 1983 when Ros Kelly became the first female member of the House of Representatives to give birth while in office; more than a decade later, in 1995, Jacinta Collins became the first senator to do so. Since then, the increasing number of women having babies while in office has meant that parliament has had to consider how it treats members who are trying to balance being caregivers for young children with doing their job in a workplace built on traditions that did not consider family caring responsibilities. This has resulted in some rule changes, including allowing senators and members to breastfeed their babies in the chamber if they need to, and letting members who are caregiving when a division is called to use a proxy vote rather than having to drop everything and run to the chamber in the four minutes while the bells are ringing.

These changes to the established practice all happened before I became a member. While reading some of the arguments that took place in the lead-up to the changes, I noted how similar they are to the debates we are having now—how tradition, culture and privilege still clash with the realities of modern life and the push for a more inclusive and diverse parliament. Here's a sample.

In 2009, Senator Sarah Hanson-Young's two-year-old daughter was ejected from the Senate after being brought into the chamber during a vote. Senator Hanson-Young subsequently told the ABC, 'People want to see a modern parliament, they want to be able to see flexibility in the workplace that allows working parents to adequately balance work-life.'[22]

Around the same time, during a debate about changing the rules of the Senate, then senator Barnaby Joyce talked about the sanctity of the chamber, describing how

> there is a special place in this parliament and it is the bar of the Senate. Go past that bar and you are in the voting section of this chamber, of course the attendants can go there too. There are seventy-six people in our nation who are elected to that bar and that is an incredible privilege. Everything about going beyond that bar of the Senate must be respected.[23]

During the debate in 2007 about whether or not to adopt proxy voting in the House of

Representatives for mothers who are breastfeeding, Anthony Albanese, who was then leader of the House, said:

> The fact is that this parliament is changing. Increasingly, it is becoming more reflective of society as a whole. I think [the provision] will send a message to the public at large that we indeed recognise that working families are a reality and that working families, particularly working mothers and new mothers, have a critical role in this parliament if we are to truly be a representative parliament of Australia.[24]

To an extent, this argument about people wanting to see flexibility in the parliamentary workplace was repeated by Anika Wells in 2021 after she'd brought her twins into the chamber for a vote. The difference is that Anika was also able to reflect on how she'd been supported by her colleagues and by current practice in doing so, rather than suffering the indignity of having her children removed, or being chastised for her actions:

I had them with me in the pram, one was asleep, and we got caught in the lift when a division was called, and I knew that someone had gotten named—which means kicked out of parliament for twenty-four hours—for bringing a coffee into the chamber several years earlier, and I had an entire double pram, so I was just having absolute kittens about bringing it onto the floor of the House for a vote. But my colleagues surrounded me, walked me in. We immediately discovered that it's not very pram-friendly because there's steps down to the seats in the House … [but] it was fine! They loved it, everyone was happy to see them, everyone was so supportive, and if us doing that prompts some conversations about how else we can make parliament a bit more friendly, then that's a good thing.[25]

The parliament and our greater democracy have not fallen apart because we've changed the rules to allow parents who are caregiving to bring their small children into the chamber with them. We are confident they still won't fall apart when we take the next logical steps to make our procedures and practices even friendlier to caregivers, and through that, friendlier to women.

THE END OF IMPUNITY

Ultimately, even with better rules, structural changes and increased diversity, we won't get real reform unless the culture of impunity within parliament is brought to an end. Changing the politics of Parliament House must include being prepared to cut loose those who behave badly—the perpetrators need to get out or be removed, and those who have supported them also need to be held to account.

This is where the politics really kick in. In our political culture, claiming a 'scalp'—achieving the resignation or firing of a minister or member—is a big deal. It is characterised as a sign of a government or Opposition in crisis. In certain situations it may even precipitate a real crisis, such as when a government no longer has the numbers on the floor of the House of Representatives. It is clear from the behaviour which has now been made public that MPs who are perpetrators have tended to believe that their acts will be safely excused and kept hidden because their vote is necessary for the retention of political power—that their support is worth far more than any public approval that may be bestowed on a prime minister or Opposition leader who calls out their behaviour and sacks them. It is part of what has prevented women staffers and MPs from coming forward with allegations of criminal or bad behaviour. Why should they put themselves through the trauma of describing what has happened to them when they don't believe it's going to be acted on? It's what Brittany Higgins spoke about when she said that, when she first made the allegation that she had been raped in a minister's office in Parliament House, she felt she was a political problem to be managed.

So the most radical, the most important change we must make in parliament is to end the culture of impunity. Our parliamentary leaders must set a new standard by emphatically punishing perpetrators, even if it delivers a blow to their own party—they must harness the current discomfort with the appalling standard of behaviour in parliament and call it out whenever it occurs, then demand and ensure there are serious consequences for those who are responsible for it. Jenny and I are ready to do our part. We say publicly and loudly that any MPs who are guilty of harassment or bullying or violence, regardless of which party they're from, should face the consequences of their behaviour, and that for serious offenses, those consequences should be equally serious, including removal from parliament.

Enough is enough.

The awful fact is that women in parliament who are afraid they'll get no action when they come forward with allegations of assault, harassment or poor behaviour, are no different to women in the majority of Australian workplaces. A survey conducted in 2018 as part of the *Respect@Work* report found that roughly one in three people had experienced sexual harassment in the workplace in the past five years.

> Underpinning this aggregate figure is an equally shocking reflection of the gendered and intersectional nature of workplace sexual harassment. As the 2018 National Survey revealed, almost two in five women (39%) and just over one in four men (26%) have experienced sexual harassment in the workplace in the past five years. Aboriginal and Torres Strait Islander people were more likely to have experienced workplace sexual harassment than people who are non-Indigenous (53% and 32% respectively).[26]

So when Brittany Higgins came forward to tell her story, it wasn't only women working in parliament who began feeling more confident about telling theirs. So many women across Australia felt like they had stories to share, and so many of them felt that it was their own stories that were being denied and not heard when Prime Minister

Morrison failed to respond adequately to Brittany Higgins' allegation.

I heard this sentiment first-hand in the stories women told me when I was out and about holding street stalls in my community in the early months of 2021. Standing on the footpath outside a super-market, women would start telling me about what had happened to them in their workplaces, and they would end up in tears. When I went on the ABC News program *Capital Hill* during that March parliamentary sitting fortnight and told Liberal Senator Ben Small to stop talking over me when I was explaining how women didn't feel heard by the Prime Minister, the clip blew up my social media—women all over Australia knew that feeling of having their voice drowned out when they were speaking in public or in a meeting.

Other women began sharing their experiences of being sexually harassed when Chanel Contos, a young woman who was educated in Sydney, started an online petition about the behaviour of private school boys. This demonstrates just how early we need to be tackling issues of consent, and the dangerous gender norms and power structures that enable violence, harassment and discrimination against women.

A RESET OF ROLES

There are myriad factors underpinning gender inequality in our country, and various policy changes are needed to nurture a culture where women are respected and men do not harm them. One area that Jenny and I should talk about is how gender roles get formed and cemented in our families, in the main through caregiving, and what role politics can and should play in transforming this. As I've already explained, I'm currently navigating the exhausting landscape of caring for small children, and that means I spend a lot of time thinking about how this shapes gender roles in our community. Jenny, meanwhile, is the woman who introduced Australia's first ever national paid parental leave (PPL) scheme, and she's the mother of three adults and the grandmother of two young children.

Australia's PPL scheme is now ten years old. It provides eighteen weeks' leave paid at the minimum wage to the primary carer—overwhelmingly mothers—and two weeks' paid leave to the secondary carer, a payment known as Dad and Partner Pay. Changes made to the scheme in 2020 aim to make it more flexible by splitting it into a continuous twelve-week paid period and a thirty-day flexible paid period that can be used anytime up until a child is two. The introduction of PPL in Australia involved quite a political battle and it is an outstanding example of some women using politics and parliament to change our community for the benefit of all women.

Jenny tells me that, for her, getting a PPL policy to the point where it had gained enough support and was ready to be turned into a reality was a ten-year campaign that started when she was first elected to parliament in 1996. It involved taking on a Howard-era environment that in public debate pitted stay-at-home mothers against those mothers who worked. On the

Labor side of politics, it involved taking on conservative unions that had fixed views about what a woman's role in our society should be once she'd had children. It meant building an economic case for supporting women with paid leave, and getting support and consensus from business groups and employers. A decade on from the introduction of a national, government-funded leave scheme, it is clear that it has been an important step in helping women to be able to have a baby, to have time to recover from the birth, to care for the baby, to be economically supported, and to not have to drop out of the workforce after they give birth.

An evaluation of the scheme conducted between 2010 and 2014 found that its impact was particularly significant in encouraging women in low-paid, insecure work and those who were self-employed to extend the amount of leave they took after having a baby, most likely because they had limited or no access to paid leave before the scheme's introduction.[27] But what PPL does not do is encourage men to spend significant amounts of time out of the workforce during their children's early years. By far the dominant caregiving model in our country sees women being full-time carers throughout the beginning of a child's life, before returning to work part-time. In contrast, men's working patterns change very little after a child is born.[28]

This, of course, has a number of consequences for women. Economically, taking parental leave has a negative effect on women's wage growth, and this pay penalty only gets bigger as the length of leave increases. An analysis of the 2009 Household Income and Labour Dynamics Australia data showed that women in this country who returned to work after twelve months' parental leave were subject to an average 7 per cent wage penalty, which increased to 12 per cent over the subsequent year. This reflects a reduction in wage growth over time, with the greatest impact being felt while a mother has an infant child. In contrast, in situations where men took leave, with each month the father stayed on leave, his partner benefited from a 6.7 per cent growth in earnings.[29]

So Australian women are not just being harassed in their workplaces at unacceptable levels. They are also suffering financially when they leave the workplace to have babies. They have the gender roles of who gets to be a carer and who gets to be an earner shoved in their face while worrying about whether their careers will ever get back on track after leave and part-time work.

While Jenny and I were writing this, a disturbing piece of research came out of the Australian National University. Researchers there analysed Australian Bureau of Statistics data and found that women who violate gender norms by earning more than their male partner face a 35 per cent higher risk of experiencing partner violence than women who don't. This was present across age ranges, income groups, cultural and educational backgrounds, and country of birth. The researchers Robert Breunig and Yinjunjie Zhang told *The Sydney Morning Herald*:

Simply increasing women's economic power may not be effective in reducing violence against women and government may need to try and influence cultural change. Thinking about how to design child care policy, parental leave policy and family payments policy to allow gender norms to evolve alongside greater gender equality in work and income seems like a clear policy direction.[30]

It is deeply distressing that gender norms are so deeply ingrained in our community that when men feel their role as primary earner is being threatened, they are violent towards women. There is a clear impetus for policies and politics that reset those norms and create a new culture where we do not sharply divide work and care along gender lines. That's why Jenny and I believe it's time that Australia's PPL scheme is extended to provide greater incentives and financial support for men so they can spend time caring for their young children. Jenny made a start on this when she introduced Dad and Partner Pay, but ten years later, we must do more with it.

Research conducted by the Organisation for Economic Co-operation and Development found those countries that include a non-transferable portion of leave that must be taken by a father in their PPL schemes, have a higher uptake of men taking leave than those that don't. Unsurprisingly, the generally progressive countries of Scandinavia comprise the majority of these. When Iceland and Sweden included a non-transferable portion of leave, or a 'daddy quota', in their PPL schemes, it led to a doubling of the proportion of men taking leave. But it's not just Scandinavia that has seen an increase in fathers taking leave when it is a 'use it or lose it' proposition. In South Korea, the number of men taking leave rose more than three-fold following the introduction of a father-specific entitlement in 2007. The OECD also notes that these schemes work best when parental leave is well paid, and that fathers' use of parental leave is highest when it represents around half or more of their previous earnings. The gender pay gap means it is typically more significant regarding a family's earnings if a man takes time out of the workforce without being financially supported.

The research also tells us that men who take longer parental leave early on stay more involved in their children's lives:

Where fathers participate more in childcare and family life, children enjoy higher cognitive and emotional outcomes and physical health. And fathers who engage more with their children tend to report greater life satisfaction and better physical and mental health than those who care for and interact less with their children.[31]

That is such an important point: by having that early time where they actually get to be the primary carer, these fathers build different kinds of lifelong bonds with their children. Imagine what that could contribute to the resetting of gender roles and norms in our country, and how it could redefine the spaces we expect women and men to operate in.

Another critical part of this reset of gender norms is affordable and accessible child care. By changing PPL to add appropriate incentives for men to take time out from the workforce after a baby is born, we would change caregiving from the very beginning of a new life. But children need fairly intensive caregiving for many years after their birth, so changes to our childcare system are also required to prevent the bulk of childrearing from falling to women.

One of the things that happens when you are a parent of small children is that you spend a lot of time in playgrounds. And when you're pushing the swing, you often get into conversations about what other people's parenting routines look like. Many of the conversations I've had at the swings have involved mums telling me how it doesn't make financial sense for them to go back to work full-time, especially when they've got one child on the swing and another in the baby carrier. Some tell me the finances don't add up enough for them to return to work at all.

The data backs up my swing chats. Amanda Rishworth explains it like this:

If child care costs too much, many families make the decision that the second income earner, usually the woman, doesn't return to work full time. In addition to cost being a barrier, it is well-documented that the current child care system and its interaction with the tax system dis-incentivise the second income earner from working a fourth or fifth day in the week. A recent study from KPMG suggests mothers can face workforce disincentive rates of between 75 and 120 per cent when they undertake an extra day of work.

Take one example. A father is working full time as a builder and earning $80 000 a year, and his wife is working part-time as a teacher and earning $40 000 a year. If the wife increased her working days from three to four, her workforce disincentive rate would be 96 per cent. That is, she would only take home four cents in the dollar for every extra dollar she earnt on the fourth day. As a result, many women want to work more, but instead work part time or not at all.[32]

It's not just that women are underutilised when it comes to our workforce. The aforementioned disincentives reinforce the gender norm that a male's career and earnings take primacy, while a female's career and earnings are secondary considerations.

Which brings us to the next important policy focus in resetting gender norms at home and in the workplace: equal pay. Nearly forty years after the introduction of the *Sex Discrimination Act*, the gender pay gap in Australia is 13.4 per cent. The largely female workforce that provides essential services such as child care is underpaid. It stands to reason that we won't see men and women equally sharing caregiving and jobs until women are properly paid for their work.

Again, Jenny has been in a position to change some of this. In 2010, the Australian Services Union lodged a case with the Fair Work Commission to try to address the gender-based undervaluation of the community services sector and deliver pay increases. Two years later, the action was successful. As Jenny points out, one of the biggest reasons it succeeded was that the Gillard government was prepared to find a way to fund the wage increases.

Of course, closing the gender pay gap is unfinished work. It is something that Labor, with the numbers of women it has in parliament, continues to fight to achieve, including by arguing for the strengthening of the Fair Work Commission's ability to order pay increases for workers in low-paid, female-dominated industries, and requiring companies with more than 250 employees to publicly report their gender pay gap.

FATHERS AT HOME, MOTHERS IN PARLIAMENT

Jenny and I have both had first-hand experience of what it looks like when fathers take time out of the workforce from the beginning of a baby's life.

When Jenny had her first child forty years ago, she wasn't in parliament yet but was working as a researcher at the Labor Resource Centre in Melbourne. She wanted to keep working after giving birth, so her then boss, Brian Howe, who was a Labor MP, granted her a month's paid leave. Jenny's partner, a schoolteacher, decided he wanted to take a year's leave to look after their baby, but he had to battle an unsympathetic Education Department in order to finally be granted twelve months' unpaid leave as a father. That early experience helped shape Jenny's career and the pattern of caregiving in her family. Her two boys and her daughter grew up with a father who cooked the meals, cleaned and directly cared for them. Think about how significantly different it was back then, and still is now, for boys and girls in our community to grow up seeing their fathers do all those things.

That aspect of her family life—her partner taking on this different gender role—was something Jenny found many people didn't talk about. Throughout her career, she received lots of comments about how hard it must be for her to be away from her children so much (yep, thanks, it is hard).

Some more thoughtful people remarked on how influential it was regarding her children's perceptions of gender to see their mum do a powerful job in a powerful workplace. But almost no-one commented on how her boys' view of masculinity would be shaped by having a father who stayed home to look after them when they were young.

My partner Daniel is now doing the same thing for our newborn son, and it is still remarkable— not the community norm—that as a father he is taking a significant amount of time out of the workforce to care for our baby. The overwhelming majority of Australian fathers still spend the same numbers of hours in employment before and after having children.[33] I do believe that it is beneficial for both my baby boy and my toddler daughter to see their father in this role. I also believe it is helping Daniel to rethink how he sees caregiving and gender roles. Just the other day he told me how he found looking after a newborn unexpectedly physically demanding, how he felt tired from holding and caring for our baby all day. This is not the discussion most men have when they get together with their mates at the pub. But it is absolutely the type of discussion most women have when they get together with other new mums.

Our partners' willingness to take on these roles has also helped Jenny and I to do our jobs as parliamentarians. Journalist Annabel Crabb wrote a whole book called *The Wife Drought* about how the careers of male politicians and other men are often enabled by having wives who look after nearly every detail on the home front, while the reality for female politicians and women in the broader workforce is usually different.

I've been pretty up-front about what a difference it makes to my ability to do my job to have a partner who reduced his workload to care for our children. I spoke about it in my very first speech in parliament. I subsequently recorded for posterity in Hansard how Daniel had to learn the hard way what taking on the mental weight of caring for a small child was all about, using another speech to describe the first time he took our then baby daughter on a plane trip by himself. It was meant to be a two-hour trip and he packed his carry-on bag accordingly—just enough nappies for that period of time, and just one bottle. But the journey stretched out to around five hours, and it entailed a wet, hungry, screaming baby for a significant portion of the flight. Not a pleasant experience for him, and to be honest, he's not all that chuffed that I continually share it to make a point. But the upshot of this is that I never spend time anymore thinking about whether the baby bag is packed when we leave our house. I know he's got it in hand, because he knows how difficult things can get when it's not sorted. And I can then clear the space in my brain that was occupied with bag-packing to make way for other things, such as my responsibilities as a parliamentarian.

How powerful would it be if my workplace and Jenny's former office, the national parliament, which has recently been on show as a place that has damaged so many women, could start to model what happens when men and women genuinely share the caring burden?

I've explained how there is a significant cohort of Labor women who have given birth in the current term of parliament. This group of women is not the first to have babies while working in parliament, but nonetheless, giving birth while being an MP is still remarkable enough that we feel a responsibility to emphasise very publicly that it is possible. Once again, however, Jenny and I argue that this change shouldn't just be about women. What about the male politicians who are the fathers of new babies? How visible are they, and how prominent are they willing to be?

As I've already mentioned, around the time I had my second baby in December 2020, my colleagues Patrick Gorman and Matt Keogh became fathers to their respective second children. Significantly, they both took leave of parliament to do so, which meant that both their caring roles and their time away from the workforce were publicly acknowledged. Pat spoke in parliament about how important it was that he was able to take three months' leave, and that while it wasn't possible for men in every workplace, it should be available to more of them. We need more men in our parliament to take up a caring role and to then talk publicly about how they perform that role alongside their professional work.

I'm going to lean on Annabel Crabb's work here again. In her 2019 *Quarterly Essay*, 'Men at Work: Australia's Parenthood Trap', she notes how, when Scott Morrison and Josh Frydenberg became Prime Minister and Treasurer respectively, they both had young children—of primary school age in Morrison's case, and preschool and toddler vintage in Frydenberg's. Crabb writes:

> One can only imagine the sustained national heart attack that would have accompanied the appointment of two *mothers* of young children to these demanding jobs … However, the first joint press conference given by the two men came and went without anyone raising the question that almost certainly would have been the first asked at an all-mothers affair: 'How are you going to manage it all?'[34]

When Crabb asked both men that question, she found that their answers were not about how they managed the logistics of being both political leader and parent, but about a model for coping with or compensating for absence:

> FaceTiming every day or dining together once a week is an expression of parental love and devotion—and very important it is too—but it doesn't contribute much practical horse-power to the engine that keeps a family running. Who does school pick ups? Who remembers to take them to the dentist? What happens when they're sick? Their spouses do most of that stuff.[35]

A male colleague of mine, Andrew Giles, tells me that while he is very involved in his young children's lives, and outside of sitting periods he is responsible for getting them to and from school (including packing their bags), making them dinner, and a number of other caregiving duties, he has never once been asked in a media interview about how he balances it all. I wish he was asked. It might push into the mainstream a conversation about parliament as an ordinary workplace complete with parents, and in turn help muster a desperately needed change in gender roles and norms.

THE GENDER CARD

One of the things Jenny and I have gone back and forth on while writing this piece is what has and hasn't changed for women—and particularly for women MPs—in the period from when she first entered politics up to the present day. We acknowledge that we now have the weight of greater numbers of women in parliament. We have stronger laws against discrimination in its numerous forms, and we have more funding for services to support women. But we haven't overcome the underlying inequality and misogyny, the way men feel entitled to harm women and are confident they can do so without serious consequences. We haven't prevented young women from being harmed in our parliament. So what is it, if anything, that makes this moment—this recognition that enough is enough—any different from the other battles women have fought for decades?

For one thing, because of what earlier generations of women achieved, the women of my own cohort of MPs can be far more public in talking about our gender, and how that influences and impacts on our politics, than could Jenny and her colleagues.

As a result of the bravery of women even younger than me—Brittany Higgins and other parliamentary staffers who have spoken out; Grace Tame and her refusal to be silent—we are witnessing the unravelling of the unspoken deal around women taking a seat in the room, the deal where we have to largely shut up about the different experiences we bring.

We can now loudly refute the argument that the issues that affect women, including violence against women, are merely for *women* to be concerned about in our politics. Instead, we can demand that these issues are acknowledged and heard by powerful men as part of a national conversation and national decision-making.

We can express our fury about the appalling culture in our parliament and the devastating consequences this has had for many young women who work there. We can demand that the men of parliament step up to change that, with less worry about whether that will be dismissed as just the 'gender girl' playing 'identity politics' with the 'gender card'.

I wonder if all this, in and of itself, might be progress of a sort. We've already talked about how politics is power. Part of that power is vested in how we define our political battles in order to fight them. Having a greater capacity to talk about and define the way in which women are treated in politics and in our society more generally means we are better equipped to push for change. And with women now seeing their reality reflected in the political conversation, the calculation for male politicians when they ignore the needs and voices of women is also changing.

This is nowhere near enough, of course, but maybe it will help us get to somewhere better.

Jenny points me towards an article in *The Monthly* from 2013, when she was a Cabinet minister and Julia Gillard was prime minister. The article, titled 'Julia Gillard and the Women in Cabinet' and written by journalist Anna Goldsworthy, features Julia, Jenny and five other women who were all ministers at the time. I think it's one of the rare contemporary articles where these powerful women discuss gender and sexism in politics. In it, Goldsworthy characterises Julia Gillard's focus on delivery and her avoidance, in her own words, of being defined as our first female prime minister. Two years earlier, in a speech to the women's political network Emily's List, Gillard had said, 'I never conceptualise my prime ministership around being the first woman to do this job. I conceptualise my job as being about delivering the things that make a difference for the nation.'

In *The Monthly* article, Jenny backs this attitude: 'I think the best way of dealing with it, and I can see the PM does it in her way, is to be incredibly positive … To just keep delivering and showing that you're a great PM'.[36]

Today, Jenny says it would have been better if she and her colleagues could have called out the sexist abuse directed at Julia Gillard at the time, but she thinks they would all simply have been accused of playing the gender card. 'I wish we could have said more,' Jenny says, 'but I'm not sure we would have been able to.' Gillard has also since said that she wishes she had called out sexist coverage early on in her time as prime minister. It's impossible to know what, if anything, might be different now if they had all done so. But it fuels the urgency to make sure we do call it out now, that we acknowledge and act on the truth of Grace Tame's statement that 'we can't fix a problem we don't discuss.'[37]

~

Kate Manne ends *Entitled* by writing about her hopes for her baby daughter, what she wants for her child:

> There's a difference between stating—retrospectively, and often judgmentally—that

a woman ought to have asserted herself in some way, versus hoping that my daughter and her cohort will be empowered to do so in a forward looking manner … I want her to at least be clear about her entitlements, and to be prepared to assert them when conditions make that possible. And when they do not, I want her to feel lucid anger, and to push for structural changes, on behalf of herself as well as those who are less privileged.[38]

Jenny and I both chose parliament as the place where we would push for these structural changes. And we both believe it is an enormous privilege to have been elected to do so. Writing this book is part of our effort to say and do more.

We want more women, including First Nation women and women of diverse backgrounds, to be able to do likewise—to choose parliament as their workplace, the place where they push for change. Crucially, we want them to be safe when they do so.

We want a reset of gender norms in our community from the very beginning of life, with policies and practices that support men and women to be in caring roles and in the workforce.

We want to enact the changes that will allow Australian women to live safe, fulfilled lives.

We want to overturn the sense of entitlement and impunity that too many men still cling to. We want serious consequences for the men who harm women.

Enough is enough.

ACKNOWLEDGEMENTS

We wrote this while on Wurundjeri land. We pay our respects to elders past and present.

From Kate

My thanks to Daniel, who supported me in writing this in the same way he supports everything I do, and who picked up even more of the child care while I did it. And to our children, Harriet and Gilbert, I hope you will grow up in a world with better gender politics.

To the women of the COTD WhatsApp group, thank you for the support, the virtual eye-rolls and the workwear discussions as we navigate being female MPs.

To Jenny Macklin, thanks for constantly reminding me what could and should be achieved for our community through being elected to parliament, and thanks to all the Labor women who have blazed the trail.

Thanks also to my office staff, especially Clare Brosnan, and to my good friend and former colleague Keely O'Brien.

This book was triggered by the recent revelations of parliament as a toxic workplace. Thanks to Louise Adler for suggesting what she called 'the fastest book project in the Western world', for prompting Jenny and I to write these reflections, across generations, of our experience as women in politics. Thanks also to Paul Smitz for editing the result.

From Jenny

My thanks to all the wonderful staff who worked with me over twenty-three years in the Australian Parliament and gave so much to advance the ideas that we all care so much about, including pursuing equality for women.

Thanks to Ross, who made it possible for me to be a mother and a member of parliament. To our children Josie, Louis and Serge, and the next generation, the grandchildren Camille and Emmanuel, there is more to be done, and it falls to each of you to do your part to make our homes and communities places where love and respect are found.

And congratulations to Kate. Looking after two small children, figuring out her new role as a member of parliament and writing a book—that takes some doing.

NOTES

1   Brittany Higgins, 'Read what Brittany Higgins Had to Say When She addressed the Women's March', ABC News, 15 March 2021, https://www.abc.net.au/news/2021-03-15/brittany-higgins-speech-womens-march-parliament-house-canberra/13248908 (viewed April 2021).

2   Daniel Hurst and Katharine Murphy, 'Scott Morrison Declares It a Triumph that March 4 Justice Rallies Not Met with Bullets', *The Guardian*, 15 March 2021, https://www.theguardian.com/australia-news/2021/mar/15/scott-morrison-declares-it-a-triumph-that-march-4-justice-rallies-not-met-with-bullets (viewed April 2021).

3   Kate Jenkins, 'Accelerating Change: Gender Equality from the Household to the Workplace',

speech at National Press Club, Canberra, 20 April 2016.

4   Anne Aly, House of Representatives, Hansard, Parliamentary Business, Parliament of Australia, 18 March 2021, https://www.aph.gov.au/ Parliamentary_Business/Hansard?wc=18/03/2021 (viewed April 2021).

5   Australian Human Rights Commission, *Respect@ Work: National Inquiry into Sexual Harassment in Australian Workplaces*, 2020, p. 17, https:// humanrights.gov.au/our-work/sex-discrimination/ publications/respectwork-sexual-harassment-national-inquiry-report-2020 (viewed April 2021).

6   ABC Radio National, 'The AFL's First Female Commissioner Outlines What Parliament Should Do Next to Improve the Treatment of Women', *RN Breakfast*, 24 March 2021, https://www.abc. net.au/radionational/programs/breakfast/sam-mostyn-parliament-house-treatment-women/ 13271036 (viewed April 2021).

7   Ministers for the Department of Industry, Science, Energy and Resources, 'Interview—ABC', *7.30*, 23 March 2021, https://www.minister.industry.gov. au/ministers/karenandrews/transcripts/interview-abc-730 (viewed April 2021).

8   Susan Ryan, 'The "Ryan Juggernaut" Rolls On', *University of New South Wales Law Journal*, vol. 27, no. 3, 2004, p. 828.

9   Ibid., p. 829.

10 Sir James Killen, 'Will We Be Allowed to Wink at a Woman?', *The Courier Mail*, 22 September 1983.

11 Senate Standing Committee on Legal and Constitutional Affairs, *Effectiveness of the Sex Discrimination Act 1984 in Eliminating Discrimination and Promoting Gender Equality*, Commonwealth of Australia, 2008, p. 48.

12 Jordan Hayne, 'Labor Promises Cheaper Childcare, Billions of Investment in Electricity Grid in Budget Response', ABC News, 8 October 2020, https://www.abc.net.au/news/2020-10-08/albanese-child-care-announcement-in-budget-reply-speech/12744984 (viewed April 2021).

13 Cameron Gooley, 'Calls for More Federal Government Attention on Indigenous Women's Safety', ABC News, 31 March 2021, https://www.abc.net.au/news/2021-03-31/calls-for-federal-government-attention-help-indigenous-women/100039796 (viewed April 2021).

14 Debbie Francis, *External Independent Review: Bullying and Harassment in the New Zealand*

Parliamentary Workplace, May 2019, p. 14, https://www.parliament.nz/media/5739/independent-external-review-into-bullying-and-harassment-in-the-new-zealand-parliamentary-workplace-final-report.pdf (viewed April 2021).

15 Dame Laura Cox DBE, *The Bullying and Harassment of House of Commons Staff*, 15 October 2018.

16 UK Parliament, *Independent Determination of Complaints of Bullying and Harassment in the Commons*, 23 June 2020, https://www.parliament.uk/business/news/2020/june/independent-determination-of-complaints-of-bullying-and-harassment-in-the-commons (viewed April 2021).

17 Annika Smethurst, '"Australian First" Umpire Could Expel Victorian MPs for Bullying Staffers', *The Age*, 18 February 2021, https://www.theage.com.au/national/victoria/australian-first-umpire-could-expel-victorian-mp-s-for-bullying-staffers-20210218-p573qd.html (viewed April 2021).

18 Emma Golledge, Dianne Anagnos, Madeleine Causbrook and Sean Bowes, 'The Government's "Roadmap" for Dealing with Sexual Harassment Falls Short: What We Need Is Radical Change', *The Conversation*, 8 April 2021, https://theconversation.com/the-governments-roadmap-for-dealing-with-

sexual-harassment-falls-short-what-we-need-is-radical-change-158431 (viewed April 2021).

19 Jessica C Smith, *The Remotely Representative House: Lesson Learning from the Hybrid Commons*, Centenary Action Group, February 2021, p. 5.

20 Jacqui Lambie, 'Have I Experienced Sexism in Parliament? No. Elitism? You Bet', *The New Daily*, 19 March 2021, https://thenewdaily.com.au/opinion/2021/03/19/jacqui-lambie-sexism-parliament (viewed April 2021).

21 Kate Manne, *Entitled: How Male Privilege Hurts Women*, Penguin Books, London, 2020, p. 20.

22 Mark Rodrigues, 'Children in the Parliamentary Chambers', Parliamentary Library Research Paper, no. 9, 2009–10, https://www.aph.gov.au/About_Parliament/Parliamentary_Departments/Parliamentary_Library/pubs/rp/rp0910/10rp09 (viewed April 2021).

23 Ibid.

24 Ibid.

25 *Weekend Today*, Channel 9, 4 April 2021.

26 Australian Human Rights Commission, *Everyone's Business: Fourth National Survey on Sexual Harassment in Australian Workplaces*, 2018, p. 8.

27 Department of Social Services, *Paid Parental Leave Scheme Review Report*, June 2014.

28 Jennifer Baxter, 'Fathers and Work: A Statistical Overview', Australian Institute of Family Studies, May 2019.

29 Workplace Gender Equality Agency, 'Unpaid Care Work and the Labour Market: Insight Paper', pp. 6–7, https://www.wgea.gov.au/sites/default/files/documents/australian-unpaid-care-work-and-the-labour-market.pdf (viewed April 2021).

30 Shane Wright, 'When Women Earn More than Their Male Partners, Domestic Violence Risk Goes up 35 Per Cent', *The Sydney Morning Herald*, 30 March 2021, https://www.smh.com.au/politics/federal/when-women-earn-more-than-their-male-partners-domestic-violence-risk-goes-up-35-per-cent-20210329-p57ewb.html (viewed April 2021).

31 Organisation for Economic Co-operation and Development, 'Parental Leave: Where Are the Fathers?', *Policy Brief*, March 2016, https://www.oecd.org/policy-briefs/parental-leave-where-are-the-fathers.pdf (viewed April 2021).

32 Amanda Rishworth, 'Affordable Childcare Is the Forgotten Part of Leading Us out of the Recession', Mamamia, 13 October 2020, https://www.mamamia.com.au/shadow-minister-budget (viewed April 2021).